THE MEETING

A ONE-ACT PLAY BY
JEFF STETSON

DRAMATISTS
PLAY SERVICE
INC.

THE MEETING

It is the front suite of a hotel room. Malcom X is asleep on the couch. The room is modestly furnished with a dresser with mirror, a television, night table, chairs. There is a large window/sliding glass door that opens to a balcony which overlooks all of Harlem. This window/door is a significant part of the room which seems to be the freedom that the confines of the room seeks to deny. Malcolm X is wearing a dark gray suit which is in need of an iron. His tie is loosened at the neck. This is a restless sleep that results in Malcolm rising sharply and letting out a groan as if awakened by a nightmare. Rashad enters quickly with gun drawn. He searches the room as if looking for an intruder. But he senses that Malcolm is not in danger this time, but rather has experienced yet another restless sleep. There is a tense moment as the two men look at each other.

MALCOLM. (*Looking at the gun.*) Will you put that away.
RASHAD. (*He puts his gun back into his shoulder holster.*) Was it the same one?
MALCOLM. It doesn't matter. . .after awhile, they all start to seem the same. (*He rises and begins to stretch. Looks at watch.*) He should be here soon.
RASHAD. Wonderful.
MALCOLM. I take it you don't approve?
RASHAD. You know I don't. But since when has that made a difference?
MALCOLM. (*He looks at Rashad and smiles gently.*) Stop pouting.
RASHAD. Malcolm, why are you meeting with him?

MALCOLM.   *(Pause.)* Do you remember the first time you made love?

RASHAD.   What?

MALCOLM.   Do you remember the first time you made love?

RASHAD.   Yeah, sort of.

MALCOLM.   Why did you do it?

RASHAD.   What do you mean, why did I do it?

MALCOLM.   Was it planned? Was there a reason behind it? Or did it just happen because it was meant to. Because you knew sooner or later you would. . .because it was time.

RASHAD.   *(He thinks for a moment.)* It was mostly 'cause the woman said I could.

MALCOLM.   *(Laughs and shakes his head.)* Rashad, there's nothing romantic about you. If you weren't my bodyguard, I think you'd be alone.

RASHAD.   For all you share with me, most of the time, I am.

MALCOLM.   *(He walks to the dresser and studies himself in the mirror.)* Did I ever tell you about when I met Billie Holiday?

RASHAD.   *(Thinks he's about to hear a tall tale.)* Yeah, okay, Malcolm.

MALCOLM.   She sang a song for me. Did I ever tell you about that?

RASHAD.   *She* sang a song for *you?* Then, Louis Armstrong asked you to play trumpet.

MALCOLM.   *(He moves toward Rashad.)* No Rashad, I'm serious. She sang it for me. She walked straight up to me, ignored everyone else in the room, then she took the flower out of her hair, and gave it to me. Then, she started to sing. *(He thinks about the moment, after a pause begins to sing softly.)* *

> YOU DON'T KNOW WHAT LOVE IS
> UNTIL YOU'VE LEARNED THE MEANING OF
>   THE BLUES
> UNTIL YOU'VE LOVED A LOVE YOU'VE HAD TO LOSE
> YOU DON'T KNOW WHAT LOVE IS

(He is swaying back and forth. Rashad after listening begins to move a bit himself, until he finds himself doing a slow dance and joins Malcolm for the second verse.)

* See Special Note on copyright page.

BOTH:
YOU DON'T KNOW HOW HEARTS YEARN
FOR LOVE THAT CANNOT LIVE YET NEVER DIES
(On the word "dies," Malcolm seems to become sullen, lost in thought. He goes through with the rest of the song, but there is no movement or life in contrast to Rashad who is now lost in the song and loving it.)
UNTIL YOU'VE FACED EACH DAWN WITH
SLEEPLESS EYES
YOU DON'T KNOW WHAT LOVE IS.
(Rashad becomes aware of the mood change and looks at Malcolm who has turned away and after several moments seems to notice the phone and is drawn to it. He takes the phone, dials it, and waits.)
MALCOLM.   Hi, it's me. . .Are you okay?. . .And the children? *(He smiles, but it is a smile with more than a trace of concern.)* They always could sleep through anything. . .just like their mama . . .*(There is a quiet, painful laugh.)* Betty?. . .I'm sorry for not being there with you. You know that, don't you?. . . Next week, when I speak at the Audubon, I want you there with me. I want the whole family there. After that, we'll spend more time together. I promise. . . .Don't get so excited girl, we got enough children. *(He laughs. It seems more relaxed.)* I've got to go, he should be here soon. . .Betty?. . .I love you. *(The words come out slowly, and painfully real.)* Kiss my little girls for me. And, if you've been good, give yourself a big hug. *(He smiles, and it gradually turns to the word, "Good-bye." He cradles the phone for several moments, then places it softly in its rightful place. He bows his head slightly and quickly pounds his fist into the palm of his hand. He does this only once, and it seems to release the tension, at least, momentarily. He begins to relax and picks-up the phone again. Rashad has been the loyal observer during all of this, wishing to give his friend privacy yet there to help at the first sign. Malcolm speaks into the phone again.)* If the F.B.I. is still listening, I'm hungry . . .could you deliver some Chinese food and red soda. *(He starts to hang-up, then remembers.)* Oh. . .and hold the pork. *(Both Malcolm and Rashad look at each other and laugh. After several moments, Rashad walks toward Malcolm.)*
RASHAD.   Is everything all right?

MALCOLM. *(Nods yes.)* The children are asleep.

RASHAD. Sister Betty?

MALCOLM. *(There is a painful, bittersweet pause.)* Our house is bombed this morning, and I'm here. . .I haven't given her much have I, Rashad?

RASHAD. Do you think she would ever feel that?

MALCOLM. She would never be that selfish. But I know. I can hear it in her voice, the fear, for me mostly, but for the family too. I should be with her tonight. I should be with my children as often as possible. *(Pause.)* They should remember their daddy.

RASHAD. The *world* will remember their daddy.

MALCOLM. They won't remember me. I know that. If I could just be sure that what I represent will be remembered. That's all that's important to me. This country will do what it can to see that that won't happen.

RASHAD. This country has always tried its best to eliminate the black man. It ain't happened yet.

MALCOLM. What can be changed, doesn't need to be eliminated. *(He takes his glasses off, rubs the bridge of his nose, gently.)* I'm tired, Rashad. . . .It seems like I've been a lot of things lately . . .but whatever else I've been. . .tired has been in there somewhere. *(Pause.)* It's stuffy in here. *(Malcolm moves toward the window but Rashad rushes to stop him.)*

RASHAD. Stay away from the window, Malcolm! Please.

MALCOLM. *(He moves back toward the seat, but remains standing. Rashad cautiously opens the window, making sure that the curtain remains drawn.)* All the forces in this country couldn't protect their own President. You think it makes a difference not to be able to breathe the Harlem air?

RASHAD. It may make a difference *tonight.*

MALCOLM. Those use to be my streets, Rashad.

RASHAD. They'll always be your streets. . . .They'll just never be safe. *(Pause.)*

MALCOLM. We're in the tallest building in Harlem, Rashad. How high up do I have to be, before I'll finally be safe?

RASHAD. Just give the word, Malcolm, and we can strike back.

MALCOLM. *(Angrily.)* Strike back? Do you think I trained them in the art of self defense, so they could protect themselves from *us?*

RASHAD. Did you train them to throw a fire-bomb through your house?

MALCOLM. *(He moves slowly toward Rashad.)* I don't think it was them.

RASHAD. *(Frustrated.)* Malcolm!

MALCOLM. No, Rashad. It just doesn't make any sense. Even Elijah doesn't have the power to do some of the things that's happened recently. *(Pause.)* It's gone way beyond that. Next Sunday, at the rally, I'm going to say some things, some things that might really begin to put the heat on us. . .I'm going to say that it wasn't the Muslims.

RASHAD. And who are you going to accuse?

MALCOLM. Who else could it be? Do you think Elijah could get the French government to ban me from traveling in France?

RASHAD. You won't ever get the initials out of your mouth, Malcolm.

MALCOLM. *(Smiles.)* I'll just have to remember to talk fast.

RASHAD. We can't afford to lose you.

MALCOLM. When I can't go near that window, you already have.

RASHAD. Won't you at least cut back on some of the speaking engagements? There's no way we can manage large crowds anymore. Not when we have to watch out for people who look like *us.*

MALCOLM. Ain't no one out on those streets look like you, Rashad. You got to go *clear* 'cross the ocean, to another land, to find someone as *ugly* as you. Either that, or all the way downtown. *(Both men laugh.)*

RASHAD. Please be serious, Malcolm. . .

MALCOLM. *(Smiles.)* After the Audubon, I'll cut down. Anyway, I told Sister Betty I would be with her more often. It's the first time she laughed in months. *(Malcolm moves to the coffee table that has a chessboard already set. He picks-up one of the pieces and smiles.)* You want to play some chess?

RASHAD. No.

MALCOLM.   Why not?

RASHAD.   Because I always beat you.

MALCOLM.   *(Smiles.)* Have I become that predictable?

RASHAD.   You play as if the object of the game was to protect the pawns. The pawns are there to protect the king, Malcolm.

MALCOLM.   Maybe it's time someone protected the pawns for a change.

RASHAD.   Then the game wouldn't be chess anymore. It would be something else. Something nobody would play.

MALCOLM.   Would that be so bad?

RASHAD.   It ain't a question of good or bad. It's a question of winnin' or dyin'.

MALCOLM.   You can't sacrifice your own people and expect to win. Look at that board, Rashad. What do you see?

RASHAD.   *(He looks at it then, with some degree of regret or sadness responds.)* I see a game, Malcolm. A game we didn't invent. *(He reacts to Malcolm's disappointment.)* You don't like the rules? Fine. Neither do I. But, the only chance we got of winning is to protect the leader. Once the leader gets too far out in front, it's open season. Hell, Malcolm, even the pawns will help to sacrifice you. *(He picks-up the king from the chessboard and moves toward Malcolm.)* As long as this one piece is free and protected, the game ain't over. Whatever else you say or do, won't change that. *(He touches his friend as if he is giving one final plea.)* As long as this *one* piece has a chance. . .we *all* do.

MALCOLM.   *(Takes the king and places it back on the board.)* Rashad, we're all pawns. When we begin to realize that, maybe the old game will be over, and a new one can begin.

RASHAD.   *(Moves toward Malcolm.)* Malcolm, go home. Be with Betty. Be with your children. You don't need to do this. We've got enough problems with half the people thinking you betrayed Elijah, and the other half thinkin' you're getting soft. All this new talk about white folks not being all bad, now, you're meeting with the "King of Love". It ain't right, Malcolm. I can feel it. Nothing good can come from this.

MALCOLM.   Something good already has.

RASHAD.   What?

MALCOLM.   I asked him to come, and he said yes. And, he

never asked why. *(Silence.)*
RASHAD.   How do you know he's really coming?. . .Malcolm, what makes you think his people will just let him get on a plane and come here?
MALCOLM.   He'll come.
RASHAD.   How do you know?
MALCOLM.   Because I'd come if he called me.
RASHAD.   *(Rashad places his hand gently on Malcolm's arm.)* Do you trust him? *(Malcolm smiles, reassuredly touches Rashad's hand, then walks away slowly.)* Malcolm, do you trust me?
MALCOLM.   *(Without turning toward him.)* I don't know that I trust anyone, any more.
RASHAD.   *(Stung by what appears to be an indictment.)* I'd *die* for you!
MALCOLM.   *(Looks at him for the first time, then, without emotion.)* People who'd die for me, I trust least of all. *(Malcolm after a moment seems to realize what he has said and the affect that it has had on Rashad. He moves toward him.)* I didn't mean that, Rashad. I guess I haven't shaken the nightmare yet. *(Beat. Then, to himself.)* At least, it will be over soon.
RASHAD.   *(Surprised by the statement and a bit alarmed.)* Why will it be over? Malcolm? *(The two men look at each other in silence for several moments. The silence is interrupted by several loud knocks at the door. Rashad makes no movement toward the door and appears to be ignoring it. Malcolm studies him patiently.)*
MALCOLM.   Don't you think you ought to let him in?
RASHAD.   You know what I think. *(Rashad goes to the door and opens it. He greets Dr. King who enters, holding a small brown bag. He looks at Malcolm.)*
DR. KING.   Minister.
MALCOLM.   Doctor King. *(Pause.)* Rashad, I think you can leave Doctor King and I alone. We'll be all right.
RASHAD.   *(He pauses, uncomfortably.)* I need to check Doctor King.
DR. KING.   Check? I was "checked" once downstairs.
RASHAD.   Not by me.
MALCOLM.   *(Smiles.)* Rashad, somehow I think that's unnecessary. I'm sure I'll be safe with Doctor King.

RASHAD.   I'm sure you'd be safe with Doctor King, too, but how do I know that's him?
DR. KING.   Perhaps I could give a short speech, or an appropriate sermon?
MALCOLM.   Oh please, Doctor, not that. *(Both men laugh good-naturedly.)* We'll be okay, Rashad.
RASHAD.   Very well, if you say so. *(Pause. He begins to exit then stops.)* Oh, can I take your coat, Doctor?
DR. KING.   Why, thank you. *(Rashad helps Dr. King off with his coat, and manages to get a quick, but obvious frisk or two in as well. Malcolm gives an embarrassed glance toward Dr. King. He then takes a bag from Dr. King opens it and looks curiously at him, then a quick glance at Malcolm. He returns the bag to King and gives him a slow and mistrusting look. Rashad begins his exit having accomplished what he set out to do, and is satisfied about having done it. He stops near the door.)*
RASHAD.   I'll be just outside if you need me. *(He exits.)*
MALCOLM.   I'm sorry about that, these are troubled times.
DR. KING.   I understand. . .I suppose the bombing has unsettled everyone.
MALCOLM.   *(Smiles.)* Didn't do much for the price of real estate in my neighborhood. . . .Did anyone see you come in?
DR. KING.   No. I followed your instructions. The next time you want me to take the back stairs, I wish you could get a room on a floor lower than the seventh.
MALCOLM.   *(Laughs.)* I've seen you on T.V. You could afford to lose a few pounds.
DR. KING.   Television makes you look heavier. . .and, anyway, this stomach is in the finest sense of southern tradition and the ministry. Congregations don't warm-up to thin preachers . . .means the preachin's not good enough to receive sweet potato pies in lieu of other donations.
MALCOLM.   My congregation sells pies street to street. . .You might say it keeps them thin and the donations fat. *(Looks at the bag.)* Speaking of pies, is that your lunch in that bag. . . or perhaps a tape recorder?
DR. KING.   And why would I need a tape recorder?
MALCOLM.   Maybe you're nervous about coming out of hotel

rooms. . . .Mister Hoover does have a way of making people paranoid.

DR. KING.   I have never thought that the Lord could have made a mistake. . .but Hoover does push one's faith beyond reasonable limits.

MALCOLM.   Have a seat, Reverend. *(Dr. King places the bag on the couch, and takes a seat near the table.)* Don't you want the couch?

DR. KING.   This will do just fine, thank you.

MALCOLM.   Oh, yes. . .I forgot; you're used to sit-ins and such.

DR. KING.   I find they're generally better for your back.

MALCOLM.   Not too good for the head, as I recall.   I'm surprised you still have one with all that non-violent *action* you've been involved in.

DR. KING.   You'd be amazed how much one can take, when the purpose is clear.

MALCOLM.   Perhaps, but I think some folks just naturally have hard heads.   *(Malcolm takes his seat, directly across the table from Dr. King.)* When I was in Selma two weeks ago, I almost paid you a visit.

DR. KING.   You should have; plenty of room in the jail.

MALCOLM.   I try not to visit jails, voluntarily.

DR. KING.   I heard your speech on my behalf was very moving.

MALCOLM.   The *younger* people seemed to enjoy it. . . .In fact, if I had spoken any longer, we all would have come by the jail house. . .except we wouldn't be planning on stayin'. . . of course, there probably wouldn't have been much jail remainin' after we left.

DR. KING.   Then, I should thank you for not speaking too long. . . .Being in jail is unpleasant enough. . .having it torn down while you're there is not my idea of how to spend a Sunday afternoon.

MALCOLM.   Oh, you can thank some of your conference planners for that, if it were up to them, I wouldn't have spoken at all. . . .As it was, they spent several hours after I spoke trying to calm the crowd down.

DR. KING.   Maybe they were trying to move them in a different direction.
MALCOLM.   Calming them down certainly would have done that.
DR. KING.   Well, since you didn't visit me then, I'm visiting you now.
MALCOLM.   Yes, and I must say, I'm impressed. I didn't think you visited Northern cities too often. . . .I imagine our streets are more difficult to maneuver than those country roads you're accustomed to.
DR. KING.   If the road was meant to be traveled, it will be.
MALCOLM.   And if it's destroyed?
DR. KING.   It will be rebuilt. . . .Or it wasn't the road for us.
MALCOLM.   Still the dreamer?
DR. KING.   And you're still the revolutionary?
MALCOLM.   *(Smiles.)* Thank you.
DR. KING.   I hadn't realized I had paid you a compliment.
MALCOLM.   Ignorance is sometimes the sincerest form of flattery.
DR. KING.   If I didn't know better, I'd think you were trying to upset me.
MALCOLM.   *(Smiles.)* A man who allows himself to get hit upside the head, certainly wouldn't get upset at some mere words. *(He smiles again, somewhat more coyly, then politely speaks.)* Care for some water, Martin?
DR. KING.   No. Thank you.
MALCOLM.   Some tea?
DR. KING.   I'm fine.
MALCOLM.   *(He moves toward the dresser takes a drink of water and then takes an apple from a fruit basket. He thinks for a moment. He brings it toward Dr. King.)* I want you to eat this.
DR. KING.   No, thank you. . .I'm not hungry.
MALCOLM.   I don't care. . .I want you to eat it anyway.
DR. KING.   I don't want it.
MALCOLM.   It's good for you.
DR. KING.   That may be, but I still don't want it.
MALCOLM.   What if I make you eat it?
DR. KING.   And just how would you do that?

MALCOLM.   By force, if necessary.

DR. KING.   I'd still refuse.

MALCOLM.   You mean to tell me, you would refuse to eat this apple, even if I resorted to force?

DR. KING.   Yes.

MALCOLM.   Even if it's good for you?

DR. KING.   Even then.

MALCOLM.   You're right, Martin, you can't force people to take something they don't want. Try as hard as you can to make white folks love us, no matter how smooth you make it, the simple fact is, they just won't swallow the truth. . .even if it's good for them. *(He places the apple back into the basket.)*

DR. KING.   *(The two men look at each other in silence for a moment.)* Isn't it odd, that you should try to tempt me with an apple.

MALCOLM.   *(Smiles.)* You see the apple as a temptation. . .I see it as nourishment.

DR. KING.   We see what we want to see, I suppose.

MALCOLM.   Some of us don't see anything at all, even when it's staring right at us. For example, when you passed by the front of the hotel, did you notice a woman standing outside? She was wearing a short red dress and heavy make-up.

DR. KING.   The prostitute?

MALCOLM.   *(Nods yes.)* How old would you guess she is?

DR. KING.   Thirty to thirty-five?

MALCOLM.   *(A painful laugh.)* She's seventeen, Reverend. Although after three years on the street. . .age has no real significance. . . .Tomorrow morning she won't know how many men she slept with tonight. She can't even tell from the money she makes. Her pimp collects that right after each trick. *(Malcolm stands and moves slowly across the room.)* She's part of a larger congregation but you won't find them in any of your churches. They would curse your God if they were alive enough to curse. . .but they're dead, Martin. . .they're the living dead. They exist because they're accustomed to it and haven't thought about why they shouldn't. If they weren't used to moving so often. . .not staying in any one place too long . . .someone would have swept them away by now.

DR. KING.   I take it you have a point to all this?

MALCOLM. I know something of the living dead, young women working the streets, and their pimps. When you're around the same people everyday. . .you don't notice the change right away. . . .Then all of a sudden, you're aware . . .someone is fat or old. . .or without hope. The purpose of all this, Martin . . .is to show you the hopeless and to let you know that the number is growing everyday.

DR. KING. Do you have a solution?

MALCOLM. Unity.

DR. KING. I've never been against that.

MALCOLM. Your unity is sitting around the camp fire while the cross is burning singing, "we shall overcome". . . .If you're really for unity you'd be singing, "we shall come over"! Every time there's an injustice, we shall come over. Every time there's a black woman being frightened by a white face behind a white hood, we shall come over. . . .Every time and *anytime* there's a need to stop white people from persecuting black people, WE SHALL COME OVER! And we will stay until black people feel safe again.

DR. KING. (*Leans his body slowly in the direction of Malcolm, and very clearly and deliberately responds.*) We *also* sang, "Ain't gonna let *nobody* turn *us* around." (*The two men stare at each other. Malcolm breaks the silence.*)

MALCOLM. It really doesn't matter what the song was. Nobody ever got their freedom from singing. On the other hand, if you're prepared to do some swinging?

DR. KING. Violence? Revenge? Is that the unity you seek?

MALCOLM. I care about survival Martin. I care about the quality of that survival. No. I don't seek violence. I seek to stop it and I'll stop it by any means necessary. I have that as a duty.

DR. KING. Violence never stops violence, Malcolm.

MALCOLM. But marches do? All those people gathered together singing songs. What did that bring? A piece of legislation?

DR. KING. Yes. Birmingham got us the Civil Rights Bill and Selma will get us the Voters Rights Legislation. Every time we can expose hatred to the world, we come that much closer to making this country live up to what it says on paper.

MALCOLM.   Did that legislation help those civil rights work-
ers murdered in the south. . .or the children blown-up in their
own church? You got nothing, Martin! Nothing. . .but some
empty promises, and a piece of paper that betrayed yet
another lie in a long list of lies. . .the American lie. . .the grand
white lie. *(Pause.)* You know, I had a dream tonight.

DR. KING.   Oh?

MALCOLM.   *(Smiles.)* I'm sorry, that's your line.

DR. KING.   You may borrow it, if you chose.

MALCOLM.   This dream I had. . .we had been dead for some
time. . .the time it takes to miseducate the average American.
. . .Young black men and women didn't know who we were.
. . .They knew nothing about the movement. . .the struggle. It
was as if it had never happened. I woke up in a cold sweat,
shaking, confused. You know, Martin, I have seen my own
death countless nights, but that vision was never as frightening
as that dream. *(Pause.)* We will be sold out. . .you and I. It
might happen over a promise for a job. . .or a deal to be
supported as the new leader. It may happen any number of
ways. . .but it will happen, Martin. . . .You might even do it to
yourself.

DR. KING.   And how do you think I will accomplish my own
undermining?

MALCOLM.   *(He takes a piece of paper from the inside of his jacket.
He unfolds it neatly, and begins to read, at first, seriously, then a bit
mockingly, then finally, with some degree of anger.)* "We will match
your capacity to inflict suffering, with our capacity to endure
it. We will meet your physical force with soul force. . . .Do to
us what you will. . . .Threaten our children and we will *still* love
you. . . .Come into our homes at the midnight hour of life,
take us out on some desolate highway and *beat us* and then leave
us there and we will *still love you.* . . .Say that we aren't worthy
of integration; that we are too *immoral;* that we are too *low;*
that we are too *degraded* and we will still love you. . . .Bomb our
homes and go by our churches early in the morning and bomb
them if you please. . .and we will still love you. . . . *(Beat.)* We
will wear you down, with *our* capacity to *suffer!"* *(Pause.)* Did

you really say that, Martin?

DR. KING.   You know I said it. And, furthermore, you know the context.

MALCOLM.   The context! The context has to be insanity!

DR. KING.   Is love insane?

MALCOLM.   No! But we aren't talking about love.

DR. KING.   Maybe you need to read it again.

MALCOLM.   I try not to inflict suffering on myself more than once. . .I suppose my *capacity* for that, is not as large as yours.

DR. KING.   *(He leans forward, angrily.)* You are not before any cameras now, Malcolm! You have an audience of one, and I am not cheering. . .so, you can stop with the sarcasm and your flippant remarks!

MALCOLM.   I don't want any cameras and I don't need any audience!

DR. KING.   And I didn't come here to debate you, so you can stop the contest.

MALCOLM.   The "contest" is more than a debate, Doctor! *(Both men are leaning toward each other. Their opposite arms are extended, elbows on the table, coming to rest in an arm wrestling position. Their hands touch, by accident or impulse, and they both smile. At first the smile appears to be a sly one, then it turns to a satisfying grin, as they seem to fall naturally into an arm wrestling contest. They struggle briefly, but not strenuously. Malcolm wins and the two men stare at each other silently, for several moments.)*

DR. KING.   *(Malcolm still has King's arm pinned to the table, but without force.)* Are you satisfied?

MALCOLM.   *(Letting King's hand go.)* I wish it were that easy, Doctor.

DR. KING.   Why is it that every time you say the words "Doctor" or "Reverend" I have the distinct impression I should feel insulted?

MALCOLM.   *(Laughs.)* I imagine it's my street accent. . . .Having not had the advantage of university training, my words sometimes appear too harsh.

DR. KING.   You're being too modest, Malcolm. It's doubtful that Harvard invites someone to lecture who has difficulty being understood.

MALCOLM.   They didn't bring me there to lecture. . . .They brought me there to be embarrassed. . .but then I don't embarrass easily. . .and since Harvard didn't have anything I wanted. . .I never saw a reason to apologize for not having it. . . .Of course, there were an ample number of Negroes there who seemed to have an abundance of apologies all saved up for just such an occasion.

DR. KING.   Do you see me as that kind of Negro?

MALCOLM.   No. . .but I see you being used by white folks, whether you intend to be or not. Which is why they'll erect monuments to you before you're through.

DR. KING.   Oh, I don't know about that. . . .Seems like the mention of your name is likely to cause a great deal of attention. . . .They may even name whole cities after you.

MALCOLM.   You got the award, Malcolm.

DR. KING.   Yes. . .on behalf of all of us. . . .People everywhere who fought against injustice.

MALCOLM.   White people gave you the award, Malcolm. . . .Doesn't it worry you just a little that the people who are doing most of the oppressing are also giving out all the awards? I think you must have impressed them most when you said, "If blood has to flow on the streets. . .let it be ours." . . .Hell, every cracker in the South would have chipped in to buy you an award for that one!

DR. KING.   The award was for *peace*, Malcolm.

MALCOLM.   No, Doctor, the award was for getting beaten and not fighting back.

DR. KING.   I didn't expect acceptance from you, Malcolm. . . .A little understanding would be sufficient.

MALCOLM.   You want me to understand how a black man would ask his people to be the first, last, and only ones to bleed? To give their precious blood, let it spill to the pavements of these cities, or sink into the soil of this nation, the nation we helped build? You want me to *understand* that?

DR. KING.   Did it ever occur to you that perhaps you were more responsible for the blood of our people flowing than I? That your speeches are unwittingly causing violence?

MALCOLM.   No! Not once! Not ever! Aggression in the

name of self-defense is not violence. . . .It's honor. . . .We have to begin to *think* for ourselves. To *do* for ourselves. . .not let the "man" shape our values for us; 'cause he has some tricky logic. He'll make us think that defending our families is wrong. That defending our communities is violence. When the music is a tango. . .you tango. . . .Simple as that. . . .If they don't want you to tango, stop playin' the music and then maybe we can waltz. . .nice and polite like, with white gloves and black ties.
DR. KING. Don't you think we've made any progress, Malcolm?
MALCOLM. Progress? Martin, you got come concessions because I was the alternative. . . .They threw some legislation, some money, and some cracker controlled programs your way in hopes that non-violence would win out. Except, we were the only ones to remain non-violent. *(Pause.)* If they kill me first, you'll have nothing to negotiate with. If they kill you first, they can't let me live. They'll make you into a martyr, Martin. They'll hold your non-violent methods up to the world as a testament to your courage. If they hold it up long enough, people won't even notice the contradiction, you were *killed* preaching it. We can't learn anything from martyrs anymore, Martin.
DR. KING. Jesus was a martyr.
MALCOLM. Two thousand years ago it was possible to die and not kill a movement. . . .Today it's brought to you in living color. . .flashed across the big screen and the small all with the same clear and unrelenting message, "when you lead, you die." When you lead, you die. How long will we continue teaching that to our children? *(Dr. King walks toward the window and stares outside. Malcolm, who is now seated, looks silently at the floor. He looks at King who turns and approaches him.)*
DR. KING. Malcolm, I have no martyr complex. I want to live a long life. I want to see my children grow-up, I want to do all the things a father is supposed to do. But, if I have to die, so that my children don't face a spiritual death, so that this country is forced to confront its own unjustice, then I'll do that. *(Beat.)* Jesus gave this movement a spirit two thousand years ago. . . .Gandhi gave it a method. Today, black people in this

nation will forge that spirit with that method and create a weapon of love. We will live as brothers, Malcolm, or we most certainly will perish as fools.

MALCOLM.   This ain't the country Reverend. . . .They stack families on top of each other out here. . .black man on top of black man. . .'til there's no room. . .'til you can't breathe. . . .When you can't breathe you either die, or you strike out and someone else dies. . . .And, the women, it can be a curse to be young and attractive out there on those streets. . . .And then, Martin, there's the drugs. . . .You put enough drugs out there, and they'll dream anything. . . .Why, they'll even believe your dreams, Doctor.

DR. KING.   I can't change, Malcolm. I think you know that.

MALCOLM.   Everyone can change. That girl in the street changed. Three years ago, she was fourteen, today she. . .

DR. KING.   I *can't* change! *(Malcolm takes his glasses off, massages the bridge of his nose and gradually his temple. He puts his glasses back on and looks at Dr. King, who has turned away from the window and moves back toward his seat.)* *(Softly.)* Neither can you.

MALCOLM.   If you can't change, can you at least get angry?

DR. KING.   *(He looks at Malcolm, and then turns away, lost for a moment in thought.)* The first march I ever led. . .I was surrounded by all kinds of people. . . .Old women, who found it hard to walk across the room, somehow found strength to march for miles. . . .Young men and women carrying their children. . .older children holding the hands of their younger brothers and sisters. . . .All of a sudden a bottle was thrown from the middle of a crowd of whites. . . .We shouted "duck"! And all the adults did. . . .But children. . .children have a need to know what's being done. . . .The bottle struck this young child. . . .It cut the whole left side of her face. . . .None of us really had time to be angry then. . . .We rushed to protect her. . .to console her. . .to worry about stopping the bleeding. . .but we marched on. *(King is speaking with a sense of emotion that makes Malcolm realize he is reliving that moment, with all the pain and fear that must have existed.)* Then, a few moments later, this huge white man. . .bigger than the truck he must have been driving that night. . .this man with all his force yelled: "Go home you

little NIGGER BASTARD"! He was screaming at this young boy, couldn't have been older than seven or eight. . . *(Pause.)* I saw the look on this child's face. . . .He was scared. . .and hurt, and maybe most of all, ashamed. He thought he must have done something terribly wrong to have all that hate directed toward him. . . . *(Looking directly at Malcolm.)* Yes, Malcolm, I can get angry. . .with all the history that makes me a black man. . . I can get angry. . . .But it's a different kind of anger. . .an anger that makes you know you can't stop lovin'. . .can't stop believin'. . . .It's an anger that makes you want to prove hate wrong.
MALCOLM.   *(Beat.)* I just want to prove hate less powerful.
DR. KING.   We both deal with power, Malcolm. We just do it differently.
MALCOLM.   Yes. You see our children bleeding and in tears and you seek to comfort them. . . .I see the man who has the rock in his hand and I seek to stop him. . . .If I can't stop him before he throws it. . .I'll see to it that he never throws another.
DR. KING.   And what will that accomplish, Malcolm? If you stop that one, there will just be another, and another, and another.
MALCOLM.   Martin, when the Russians brought missiles into Cuba, Kennedy didn't ask people to turn the other cheek and pray. He didn't try to fight the Russians with love. No. He got himself some bigger missiles and told 'em to pack-up and get out. He was prepared to use force to protect this country and this country expected him to do that. I'll tell you something else, Martin, the Russians respected him, that's why they left.
DR. KING.   And missiles are still being built all over the world. Do any of us really feel protected?
MALCOLM.   You can't see the contradiction, can you? Even when you marched, you needed the protection of the federal government. It took the entire national guard to enroll one Negro in college. What did you think those tanks were there for, to help the students with their books?
DR. KING.   Those tanks were there because this movement needed to hold a mirror in front of this country and through our pain reveal its injustice.

MALCOLM.   Doctor, it doesn't matter how good a football player you are, when the game is baseball you better get yourself a bat. And if you've got problems swinging it, you ought to stay out of the game.

DR. KING.   Somehow, I had hoped that your trips to Mecca had given you a greater vision than that, perhaps even a broader compassion.

MALCOLM.   You don't tame the lion and leave the jungle unchanged, Martin. Yes. I saw things outside this country, *outside* this country. Saw things that perhaps my heart wouldn't or couldn't let me see before. I saw whites, who when they talked about color, made it seem incidental; like describing a suit or a sunset. But here, *(Smiles.)* here, it's different. When the "Man" here talks about color, you know what he means. You hear it in his voice, see it in his expression. He means he's on top and you're not. And there's no way he's gonna let that change. It's a simple question of power and privilege. And the one in power, always decides the privilege. *(He touches King's arm slightly.)* We aren't the ones in power, Martin. And we won't be until we gain control of our own lives, our own thinking.

DR. KING.   You want to free blacks. I want to free America. It's the only way any of us can be free, Malcolm.

MALCOLM.   *(Frustrated.)* Martin, can't you see what's happening to us? Five years from now, ten at the most, whites won't have to do anything to us. We'll be doing it to ourselves. Some of the brothers who sit peacefully in your demonstrations, and have their heads split open, do you know they go back to their *own* communities and commit violent acts. It's the *rage*, Martin. It's the *hurt* that's all balled-up inside and makes you strike out in the only way you can. . .the only way that's acceptable. *(Pause.)* I can't free us from that rage. . .but at least I can try and direct it to the right source.

DR. KING.   Don't we really want the same things, Malcolm?

MALCOLM.   You want us to be able to buy a cup of coffee . . .I want us to be able to sell it. . . .You want us to integrate the coffee shop. . .I want us to own it. . . .You want white folks to hire us. . .I want us to be able to hire ourselves. . . .No, Martin . . .we do not want the same things. . . .I'm afraid your quest

for integration will be the white man's solution for control.
. . . Maybe the only hope we have is that they'll hate us so much
that they won't recognize the power they'd have over us, if they
just let us in.

DR. KING.   And so, those of us who don't agree with your
definition of power and control. . .I suppose we are to be called,
"Uncle Tom's"?

MALCOLM.   I only refer to the *older* ones as "Uncle". . .and
I don't call them "Tom" anymore. . .I call them "Roy" or "Ralph"
or "Uncle Whitney".

DR. KING.   They don't deserve that from you, Malcolm.
. . .They don't deserve that from anyone. Do you think the
unity you seek can be achieved through insult and ridicule?

MALCOLM.   *(Innocently.)* Have I "ridiculed" you, Reverend?

DR. KING.   Did you think I should be flattered at the term,
"Reverend Doctor Chickenleg"?

MALCOLM.   It was, "Chickenwing" to be more precise. Would
you have found it more flattering if I referred to you as, "De
Lawd"?

DR. KING.   *(King begins to roll up his sleeve.)* "The Movement"
would have been sufficient.

MALCOLM.   *(Smiles, while taking his jacket off.)* Isn't it wonderful how well the two of us are getting along?

DR. KING.   I suppose it's time for a rematch?

MALCOLM.   So there is an ego there to bruise. You should
feel fortunate that a rematch is possible. . . .Oh well, my friend,
I am prepared to inflict suffering if you are prepared to endure
it. *(Both men smile. It's a smile less sly and more respectful than the
first contest, but still manifesting a degree of distance. After a brisk
encounter, King emerges the winner.)* Well, it seems we are even,
Reverend.

DR. KING.   Yes. I suppose we are. Is that why you invited me?

MALCOLM.   Actually, I'm surprised you accepted the invitation.

DR. KING.   I came because I wanted to offer my protection.

MALCOLM.   *(In disbelief.)* What?

DR. KING.   When I heard about this morning, I thought you
. . .

MALCOLM. *(Laughs.)* Protection? You? Offer me. . .protection? *(Angrily.)* And how are you going to do that, Sir. Are you going to have a mass sit in and pray? Or perhaps your non-violent *action* movement will frighten the Molotov cocktail throwers so much that. . .

DR. KING. *(Angrily.)* Any Molotov cocktails that were thrown through your house, were thrown there because of *your* movement, Malcolm, not mine!

MALCOLM. Yes, Doctor King, *my* movement is *flexible.* It considers *all* options! It rules *nothing* out! Its one goal is *freedom* Absolute. Total. And complete. It doesn't ask. It doesn't beg. It takes. It's willing to pay the price for freedom. Those that aren't willing to pay for it really don't want it.

DR. KING. Don't set yourself up as the authority on freedom, Malcolm!

MALCOLM. Why, I wouldn't think of it, Reverend. "Authorities" are those who study so hard to be white. If they do real good, they get to be "scholars" and if they speak for all Negroes, they get to be called "authorities"!

DR. KING. I came here to offer my help, Malcolm, if you don't want it I can. . .

MALCOLM. Your help? You're helping to kill me, Doctor!

DR. KING. Am I to be accused of that too?

MALCOLM. Not accused. Indicted! This non-violent movement of yours will get us all killed.

DR. KING. Non-violence is the only chance we have, Malcolm. By appealing to the conscience of this country. . .

MALCOLM. The conscience of this country!? This country has no conscience. It has no morality, no sense of honor! Hell, Martin, it doesn't even have a memory. It forgets what it doesn't want to remember and what we won't let it forget it lies about. This country only has a conscience when you agree with it. It doesn't care about right or wrong. It just cares if you agree with it. And if you agree with it, it agrees with you. It calls you a hero when you tell black people to be non-violent here, but it would call you a liar and a coward and a traitor if you told those same black people to stop dropping napalm on brown-skinned babies in Viet Nam. You think you can appeal to the conscience of a country like that? *(Beat.)* The Jews in Germany were non-violent, Martin. They remained non-violent all the way to the gas ovens. Go ask the victims who survived the concentration camps if non-violence got them their freedom. As for me, I'm going to deal with the victims of the concentration camps we have in America, except here they're called, New York City, or Detroit, or Philadelphia, or Chicago. *(Pause.)* No, Martin. If you're looking for a conscience, you better look some place else. Anybody who preaches non-violence while they see the man out there building gas ovens, is helping to destroy his own people. And, when black people refuse to fight back, it not only becomes easy for racists to kill us, it becomes justifiable.

DR. KING.   And you think I've contributed to that?

MALCOLM.   Let's just say, anyone who wants to kill me, anyone who wants to kill any black man, does not have to stop and think about the consequences of their actions. They don't stop to ask: "Now, what would the good Doctor, do?" They know what you'll do. Nothing! Which is about what you've accomplished. Nothing.

DR. KING.   *(He looks at Malcolm, at first with anger, and then with disappointment.)* Don't tell me that we haven't accomplished anything, Malcolm. That people get beaten for nothing. Do you really think that it is easy for me to see our own people beaten? To sit there and risk the lives of my children? Malcolm, do you think I would risk my own life for nothing? I don't want to die. I don't want my people to die. I don't preach non-violence because I like it! I preach it because it's right. And, because I'm a man. And, because I'm a child of God! *(He moves to the window.)* You look out over this city, and see neon signs that tell you what to do, and where to go. But I grew-up with a different kind of sign. It wasn't neon light, but if you were black, you had no trouble seeing it. Signs of separation. Signs that burned the words "for colored only" in the psyche of Negro children. Signs that degraded and humiliated those children's parents on a daily and constant and continuing basis. *(He moves toward Malcolm.)* When those signs came down, the spirit of black people went up, so, don't

tell me *nothing* was accomplished. *(Beat.)* I was in a Montgomery church, when the announcement was made that busses in Alabama, would no longer be segregated. What was accomplished was written on the faces of those who struggled so long to prove you could take a stand by sitting down. No, Malcolm, the only ones who doubted that we had accomplished anything, were those who never had to get up to give their seat to a white person, or move to the back of the bus, or watch white patrons being served in the comfort of a public restaurant while being forced to take food out into the rain or cold. Don't diminish what was accomplished and don't misunderstand what will be accomplished. Sometimes you got to be able to ride the bus before you can drive it, Malcolm. But don't think that we're not planning to own the whole bus line, one day. *(Pause. Then, he moves very close to Malcolm.)* And, Malcolm, don't ever mistake non-violence for non-action. You do a disservice to those who have been beaten, so that you might have the freedom to question their courage.
MALCOLM. *(Beat.)* I have never questioned their courage, just their judgment.
DR. KING. I'm beginning to question my own for coming here.
MALCOLM. Well, that can be easily corrected, Doctor. The same steps that brought you here, will lead you away.
DR. KING. On that, we can at least agree.
MALCOLM. Yes! Yes, we can! *(He moves toward the door.)* Rashad! Rashad! *(Rashad enters.)* Get a driver for Doctor King. He wishes to leave.
RASHAD. It will be my pleasure. *(He exits.)*
MALCOLM. Have a pleasant trip home.
DR. KING. *(King gets his hat and coat.)* I shall. Thanks very much for the lecture on unity.
MALCOLM. You're welcome. And before you go, you should know this, my faith teaches me not to embarrass even my own enemies. I let you beat me in arm wrestling the second time.
DR. KING. My faith teaches me to show mercy, especially to my enemies. I let you beat me the first time. It seemed the Christian thing to do. *(King begins to move toward the door as*

Malcolm spots the paper bag and picks it up.)
MALCOLM.   You forgot your lunch.
DR. KING.   It's not mine. It's a gift.
MALCOLM.   *(He opens the bag and removes a black doll. He looks at it suspiciously and then says sarcastically.)* Is this what you brought me for protection? Does it possess some kind of magical powers? Or is the doll non-violent too?
DR. KING.   It's not for you. It's for your daughter. My family was watching television when the news bulletin about the bombing appeared. They showed a film report of the damage to your home. You were on the front lawn holding one of your daughters.
MALCOLM.   *(Softly.)* Attallah?
DR. KING.   Yes. My daughter wondered if everything in the house had been destroyed. When she learned that I was going to see you tonight she thought Attallah could use a friend. That's her favorite doll. She loves it very much. If it has any "magical powers" I suppose it's because of that.
MALCOLM.   *(For the first time, he is unsure and obviously taken aback by the kindness as well as his own actions.)* What's her name?
DR. KING.   I don't know that she has one.
MALCOLM.   *(Smiles.)* I meant your daughter's.
DR. KING.   *(Chuckles.)* Yolanda.
MALCOLM.   How old is she?
DR. KING.   Nine.
MALCOLM.   Attallah is six. She'll love this. *(Pause.)* Thank your daughter, thank, Yolanda, for her. . .for both of us. *(The two men stare at each other briefly, somewhat awkwardly and yet with a sense of tenderness brought on by the moment. King nods approval or possibly, goodbye, as he turns to exit. Malcolm quickly and loudly says:)* Doctor King!. . . *(There is a pause as the two men face each other again.)* Martin, you've been to the mountain top. If you have a moment, I'd like to share mine with you. That could be my gift, to you.
DR. KING.   *(Smiles.)* I could hardly refuse an offer like that. *(Malcolm moves to the balcony, slides the window back, and motions for Dr. King to step out with him.)* The balcony?
MALCOLM.   I want you to see, what I see.

DR. KING.   From out there?

MALCOLM.   What's the matter, Reverend?

DR. KING.   I've never been partial to heights.

MALCOLM.   You're afraid of high places, Martin?

DR. KING.   I didn't say I was afraid. I just said I wasn't partial.

MALCOLM.   *(Malcolm starts to laugh. But it is clearly the type of laughter and teasing that is shared among friends.)* Well, don't that beat all?   *(Malcolm moves out onto the balcony and seems relieved to be able to breathe.)* The problems all seem smaller from here, Martin, more manageable.   *(Malcolm beckons King, who moves tentatively toward him. They stand side by side, looking over the streets of Harlem, in silence.)* It may not be the country, Reverend, but there are some things you can love more than the land.

DR. KING.   Like the people who live on it?

MALCOLM.   Yes, Martin, the people. *(There is a pause, as the two men look at each other. It is a tender look, one of admiration and concern.)* Would you do it again, Martin? If you had the choice, would you do it all again?

DR. KING.   Again? I didn't want to do it the first time. . . .I wanted to lead a church, not a movement. But, then a woman took a bus ride. . . .It's amazin' what you'll do once your feet get tired.

MALCOLM.   *(Laughs.)* You know what I wanted to be?. . . A lawyer.

DR. KING.   For the prosecution or defense?

MALCOLM.   Doesn't matter, either way I would have been held in contempt. *(They laugh.)*

DR. KING.   Makes no difference what they call you. Just matters what you answer to.

MALCOLM.   *(Pause.)* You know, it's ironic, you tried to stop whites from hating us, and I tried to stop us from hating ourselves. We'll probably be killed by those we tried so hard to teach.

DR. KING.   Why did you really want to see me, Malcolm?

MALCOLM.   *(Softly.)* I don't know. . .I suppose I wanted to see if you'd come.

DR. KING.   Another test?

MALCOLM.   No. . .another chance. Another chance. *(Pause.)*

Did you really come here to offer protection?
DR. KING.   Maybe I should have said, comfort. . .the type of comfort one man can give to another.
MALCOLM.   Do you think that people will remember us as "men" and only "men"?
DR. KING.   No. And we can't afford to let them know that that's all we are. At least, not for awhile.
MALCOLM.   Have you ever wondered what type of men we would have been, had we been born in a different time. . . .You know, a time when race didn't matter. . . .Where injustice was just a part of a history lesson.
DR. KING.   I imagine we would have been quite dull.
MALCOLM.   (Laughs.) And we would have grown very old.
DR. KING.   The dull have a way of outliving the rest of us . . .perhaps that's their greatest punishment.
MALCOLM.   Punishment. . .my father was murdered because he spoke out. . .my mother was institutionalized, because some pain deep inside of her drowned out the language of the world. . . .I have nothing to leave my own family, no money, now not even a home. . . .And yet, I still wonder, was there more I should have done. . .more of myself I could have given?
DR. KING.   My father use to tell me the story of a young Baptist minister who had gone North to seek his fame and fortune. After he had become very successful, the Pastor of his former small southern church extended an invitation to return home for a visit and preach before his old congregation. Well, this minister could hardly refuse such an offer, in fact, he was rather proud at the thought of coming back and showin' the folk how successful he had become. He decided to bring his seven year old son with him, to teach him a lesson about his history. . .his roots. . . .When the minister returned to his old church he was moved so much, that he proceeded to give one of the best sermons of his life. . .had the congregation rollin' from one emotion to another. When it was all over the Pastor threw his arms around the young minister and said: "John, that was a truly moving and inspirational sermon. . . .I wish we could give you some kind of honorarium, but as you know, our

church is not doing so well." *(Both Malcolm and King laugh.)* John just waved the Pastor off and said that was fine, it was payment enough simply to return home for a visit. As John and his son were leaving, they passed the church collection box. John stopped and took out a crisp new ten dollar bill and placed it in the box. He and his son then proceeded out of the church to the parking lot. As they were getting into the car all of a sudden the Pastor came running outside calling John's name. As the Pastor caught up to John he said: "I know you don't want any payment, but we just couldn't let you leave without at least a token of our appreciation." The Pastor handed John a crisp new ten dollar bill which John immediately recognized as the one he placed in the collection box, just moments before. He took the money, exchanged final farewells with the Pastor and got into his car. After a moment or two, he looked at his son, smiling proudly and confidently and said: "Son, I hope this teaches you a lesson." His son nodded, looked at his father and said: "Yes dad, it has. If you had given more, you would have gotten more." *(Malcolm laughs, but Dr. King smiles sadly. He gives a quiet and distant look, then softly to Malcolm he says:)* We all have to give more, Malcolm. . . .More than we thought we needed to. Even then, sometimes it's not enough.

MALCOLM.   We may both give our lives for this thing we call, "freedom". You know that, don't you? *(The two men look at each other, Malcolm then turns toward his streets having received the only answer he could. Dr. King begins to think of something that brings a faint smile which turns to an amused laugh. Malcolm seems surprised by this sudden change in mood.)* What's so funny?

DR. KING.   I was just wondering what Coretta might think, if she knew we spent the night arm wrestling.

MALCOLM.   *(He thinks about it then laughs, too.)* I suppose if Betty knew, she'd go into early labor. *(They both look at each other and laugh more loudly.)*

DR. KING.   When is she due?

MALCOLM.   *(Shrugs.)* You know about babies, Martin. . .they come when they want to. Whether you're ready, or not. *(There is a tender moment as these two men think of their families.)* Martin,

can you keep a secret?
DR. KING.   Who, me? *(They both laugh.)*
MALCOLM.   I'm hoping for a son, this time. *(Malcolm moves into the room, King after a beat, follows. Malcolm picks-up the doll, smiles.)* And a little child shall lead them.
DR. KING.   *(Pulls the curtains together.)* And the lion shall dwell with the lamb. *(Malcolm begins rolling up his sleeves, begins to take some deep breaths, a few stretching exercises, and places the chairs in order. King watches him curiously.)* What are you doing?
MALCOLM.   *(Smiles.)* I suppose we ought to declare a winner.
DR. KING.   *(Smiles.)* Yes. . .I suppose we should. If there can't be a truce, at least there ought to be a winner. *(King begins to take his coat off, rolls up his sleeves, loosens his tie, and begins deep knee bends.)*
MALCOLM.   We're arm wrestling, Reverend, not racing the relays.
DR. KING.   You warm-up the way you want to, I'll warm-up the way I want to. *(Malcolm studies him for a moment, then decides he too should do some knee bends. Malcolm is exercising in unison with Dr. King, but out of King's vision. Both men, when warmed-up move toward the table for final contest, and loosen their ties and shirts to have maximum comfort.)*
MALCOLM.   Don't take advantage of me, Reverend. . . . Remember, I'm older than you.
DR. KING.   The public for some reason continues to think of you as younger.
MALCOLM.   They associate militancy with youthfulness.
DR. KING.   That's odd, it's rather an old idea. *(They both lock hands.)*
MALCOLM.   Some of the best ideas are.
DR. KING.   Whoever wins in here will not necessarily be the winner outside you know?
MALCOLM.   If I thought that, *I* would have invited you, a long time ago. *(Both men are now seriously into the combat. Malcolm begins to get a slight advantage.)* Beware, Doctor. . .the old man is taking charge.
DR. KING.   *(Begins to even the contest.)* "HE didn't lead me here only to have me turn around now"!

MALCOLM.   Quoting scriptures, won't help you. *(Both men are seesawing to victory.)*
DR. KING.   *(Straining a bit.)* Can't hurt.
MALCOLM.   You should fight this hard when some sheriff tries to put a knot upside your head.
DR. KING.   You think it's so easy, you should try it some time.
MALCOLM.   How long do you think we can continue this?
DR. KING.   What?
MALCOLM.   I said, how long!?
DR. KING.   Not long!
MALCOLM.   How long!?
DR. KING.   I'm willing to call it a draw, if you are?
MALCOLM.   Okay, you stop first.
DR. KING.   I'm from the country, Malcolm, but give me some credit.
MALCOLM.   All right. . .all right. . .I'll count to three.
DR. KING.   Are you going to do all the counting?
MALCOLM.   *(Still struggling.)* We'll alternate. . . .Does that meet with your approval?
DR. KING.   They taught me at school that "three" was an odd number.
MALCOLM.   Look, I'll start, you go next, and we'll finish at the same time. Agreed?
DR. KING.   Agreed. *(The two men take one last go at it. Malcolm starts to lose.)*
MALCOLM.   One! I said one! *(Malcolm starts to get advantage back.)*
DR. KING.   Two!. . .Two! *(With all their power they strain a tie.)*
BOTH.   Three. *(They both stop and let out groans of battle. They look at their hands that have gone through much punishment.)*
DR. KING.   Just imagine what we could have accomplished, if only we had joined hands and pushed in the same direction.
MALCOLM.   *(Pause. Malcolm studies King, then, softly asks:)* Martin, do you respect me?
DR. KING.   I will always be against violence, Malcolm, regardless of the cause.
MALCOLM.   *(Almost painfully.)* I asked you if you respected me, and you speak of violence. Is that all you see? *(Rashad*

enters, but remains at the door, unnoticed.)
DR. KING. *(He moves toward the window.)* You don't need to ask me that, Malcolm. Just walk out there on those streets. The eyes of the dead come alive in your presence. They believe in you, and because of that they are beginning to believe in themselves. They respect you. And, yes, Malcolm, I respect you. You would have made one fine Baptist preacher!
MALCOLM. *(Smiles warmly.)* I wish my father were alive to hear that. *(Pause.)* I suppose we will not be seeing much of each other?
DR. KING. *(He notices Rashad, for the first time.)* No. I imagine we won't.
RASHAD. Malcolm, is everything all right? We've been waiting for Doctor King.
MALCOLM. I suppose I should be letting you go. It's getting rather late.
DR. KING. Yes. It is.
MALCOLM. Rashad, you want to help Doctor King with his coat?
DR. KING. Oh, no! That's quite all right. I think I can manage by myself.
RASHAD. Wonderful.
MALCOLM. *(Laughs.)* Let me help you with that, Martin. *(Malcolm helps King with his coat. Hands him his hat.)* Rashad will accompany you downstairs. I have someone with a car, he'll take you where you need to go.
DR. KING. I appreciate that. *(They walk toward the door.)*
MALCOLM. We could have made quite a team.
DR. KING. We *do* make quite a team. . .most persons just don't realize it.
MALCOLM. *(Smiles.)* May they be ignorant a little while longer.
DR. KING. Amen to that.
MALCOLM. All praise to Allah.
RASHAD. Malcolm, do you want more time together, to exchange prayers with your friend.
MALCOLM. You don't have to be together to exchange prayers, Rashad. *(Beat.)* Particularly, with a friend.

DR. KING.   *(Smiles.)* Rashad, I'm ready, if you are. *(They begin to move toward the door, when Malcolm speaks.)*
MALCOLM.   I never meant to hurt you with anything I might have said publicly. It's very important to me that you know that. *(King stops. He turns very slowly toward Malcolm. He is obviously touched by Malcolm's words. He proceeds toward Malcolm.)*
DR. KING.   It's very important to me that you told me. *(The two men stare at each other in silence, only a few feet apart from one another. They both reach out to shake hands, but suddenly embrace. It is a tender embrace that recognizes the friendship and respect that has occurred, but also the reality that they may never see each other again.)*
MALCOLM.   Martin?. . .If you're around longer than I am, tell them we climbed one mountain, together.
DR. KING.   And, we saw the promised land.
MALCOLM.   Yes. Tell them all.
DR. KING. *(He smiles, warmly.)* Take care of yourself, Malcolm. *(King exits. Rashad watches Malcolm.)*
RASHAD.   Malcolm, is there anything I can do? *(There is no response as the men look at each other. Rashad exits.)*
MALCOLM.   Goodbye, Martin. . . .Goodbye. *(He places his hands in position for prayer.)* Allah. . .protect the dreamer. *(He smiles warmly, and then notices the doll. He picks it up and stares at it, sadly at first. Then he shakes his head. He chuckles, then laughs. He moves toward the window and looks out on his beloved Harlem. He studies the doll and begins to sing softly.)*
   YOU DON'T KNOW WHAT LOVE IS
   UNTIL YOU'VE LEARNED THE MEANING OF THE BLUES
   UNTIL YOU'VE LOVED A LOVE YOU'VE HAD TO LOSE
   YOU DON'T KNOW WHAT LOVE IS
(The lights fade gently on him holding the doll. When the rest of the stage is dark the one light on Malcolm fades quickly.)

CURTAIN

PROPERTY LIST

Pistol
Shoulder holster
Chess set and board
Small brown bag
Glass of water
Fruit basket with apples
Piece of paper
Black doll